This book belongs to:

_____

_____

SNAIL

ELEPHANT

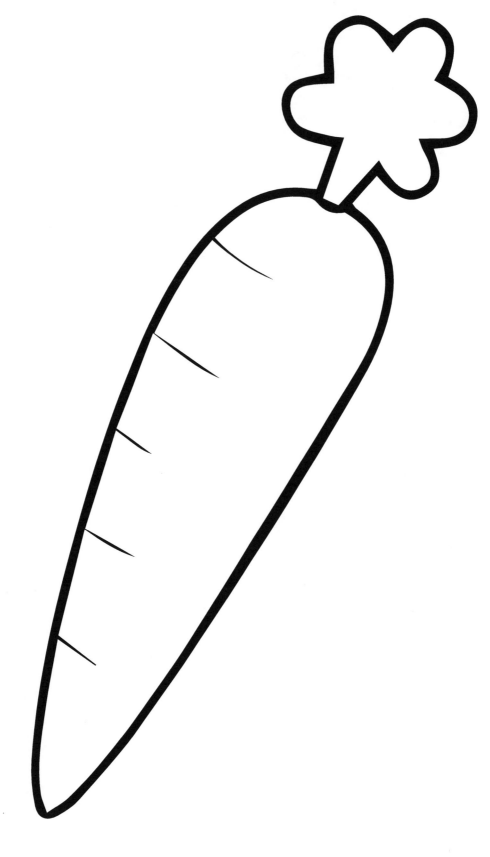

CARROT

COW

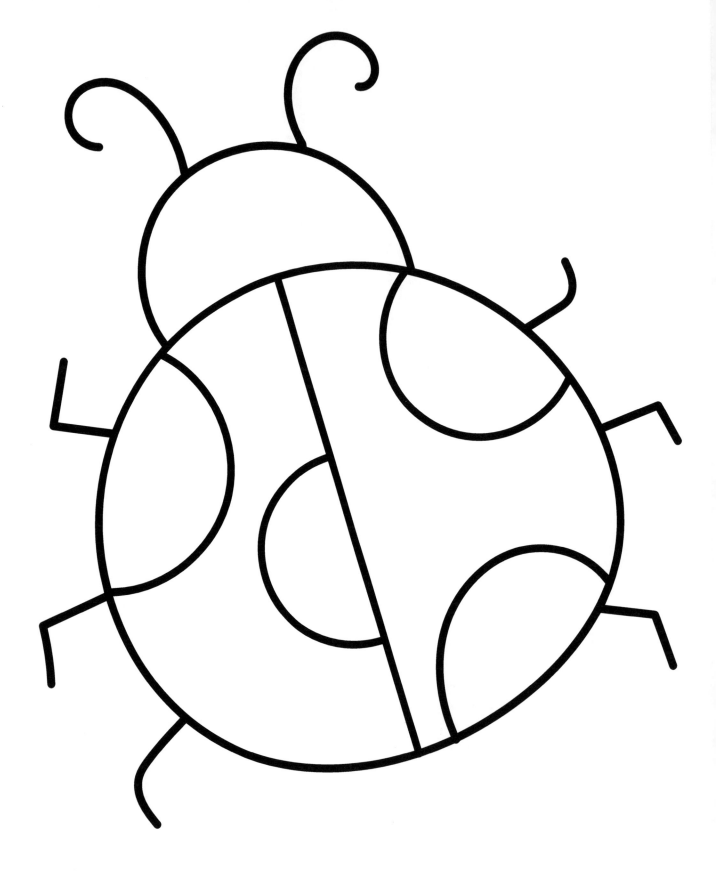

LADYBUG

CAMEL

DOLPHIN

CROCODILE

CUPCAKE

KOALA

CHICKEN

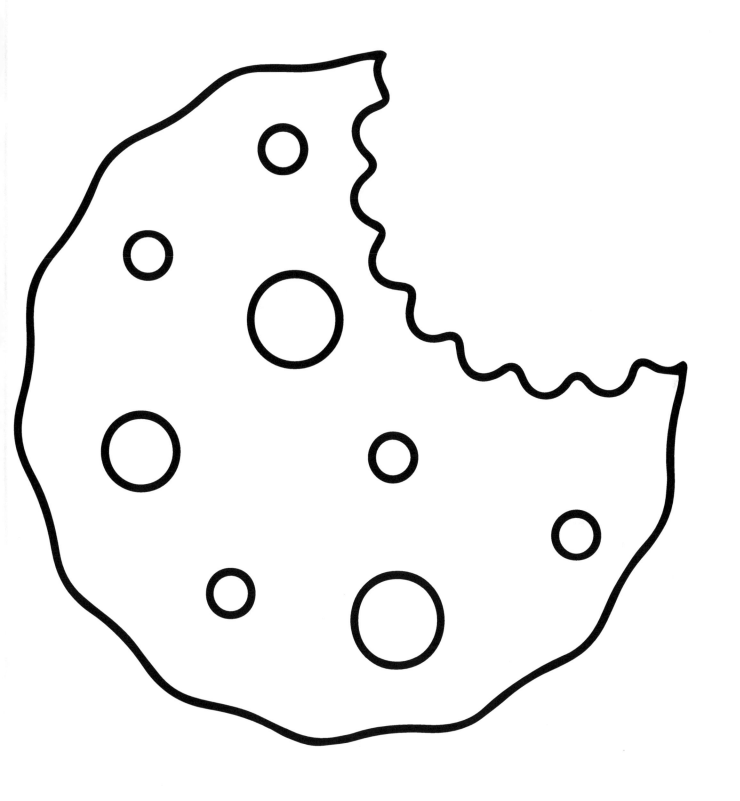

COOKIE

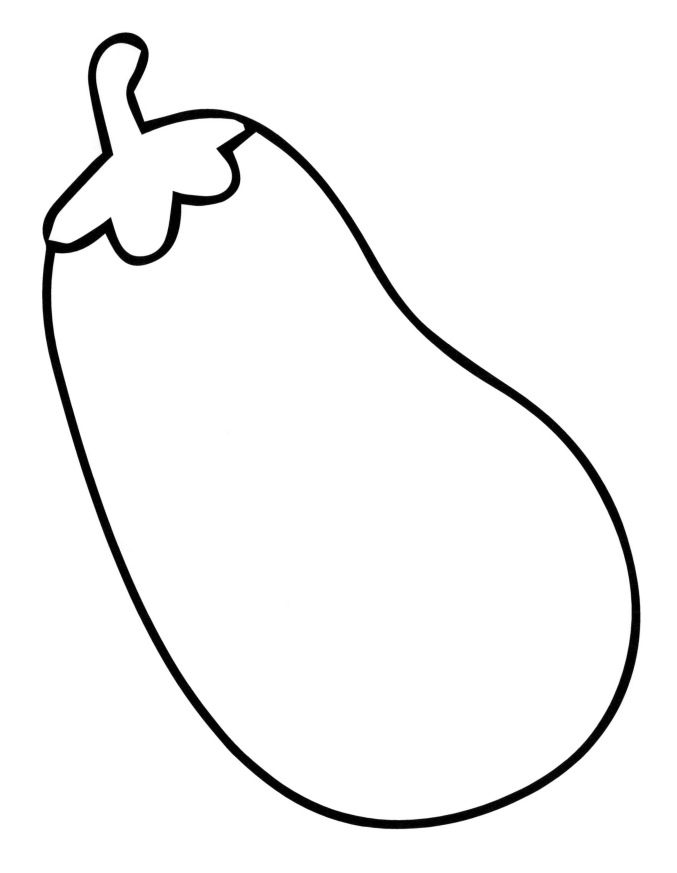

EGGPLANT

DOG

STAR

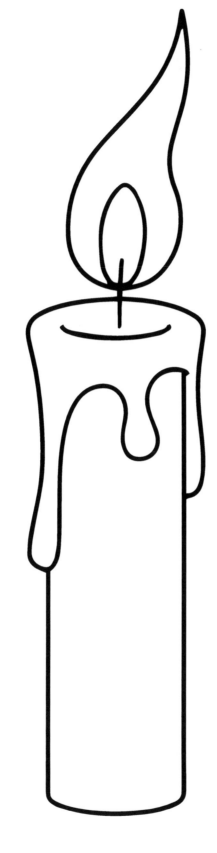

CANDLE

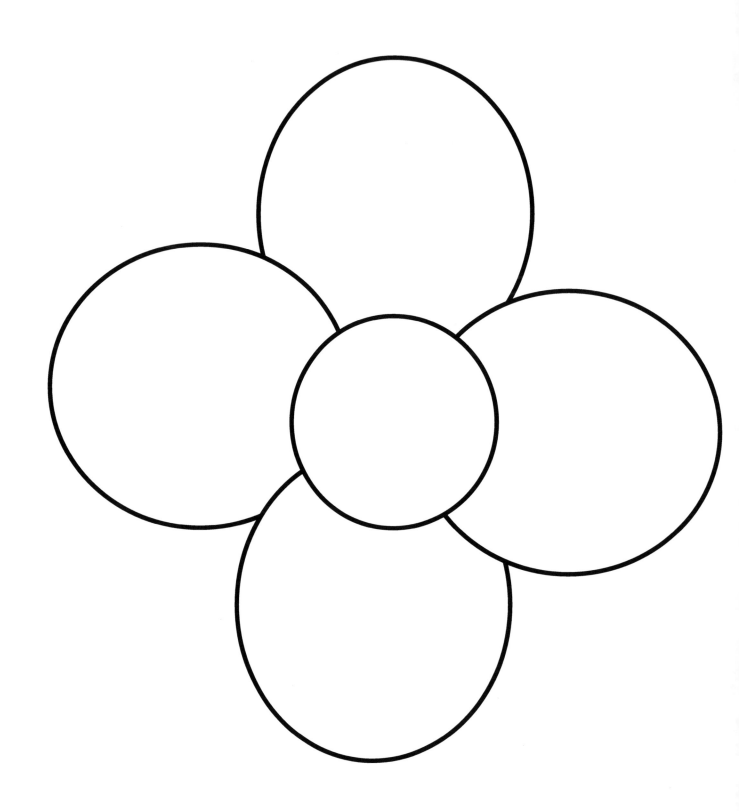

FLOWER

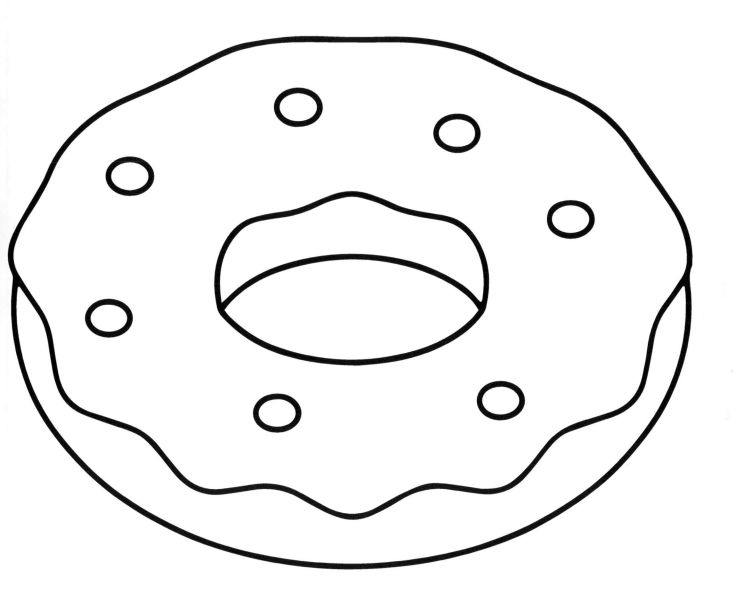

DONUT

BUTTERFLY

KANGAROO

RADISH

GOAT

ICE CREAM

LAMA

CORN

SNAKE

BIRD

REINDEER

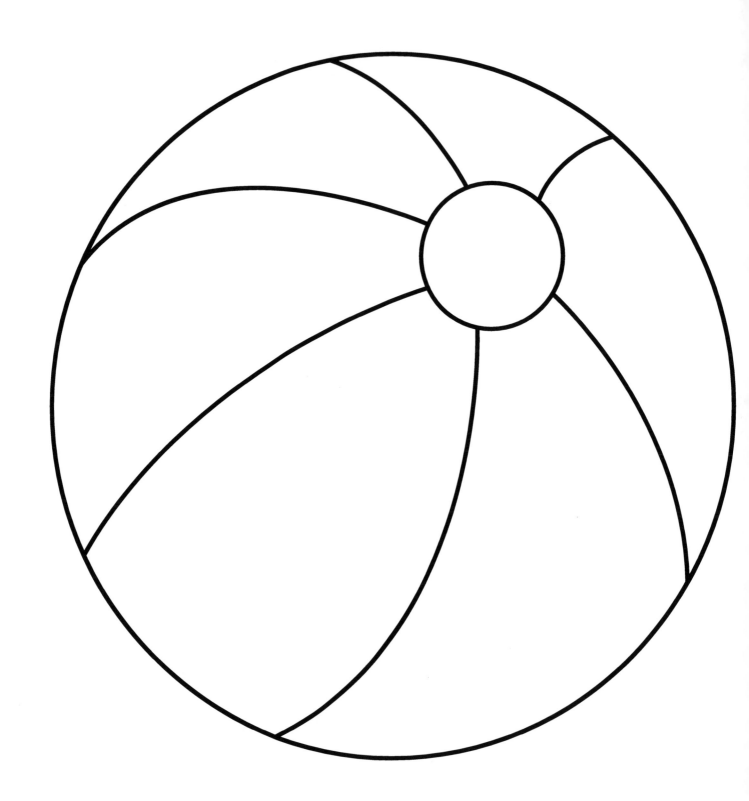

BALL

LOBSTER

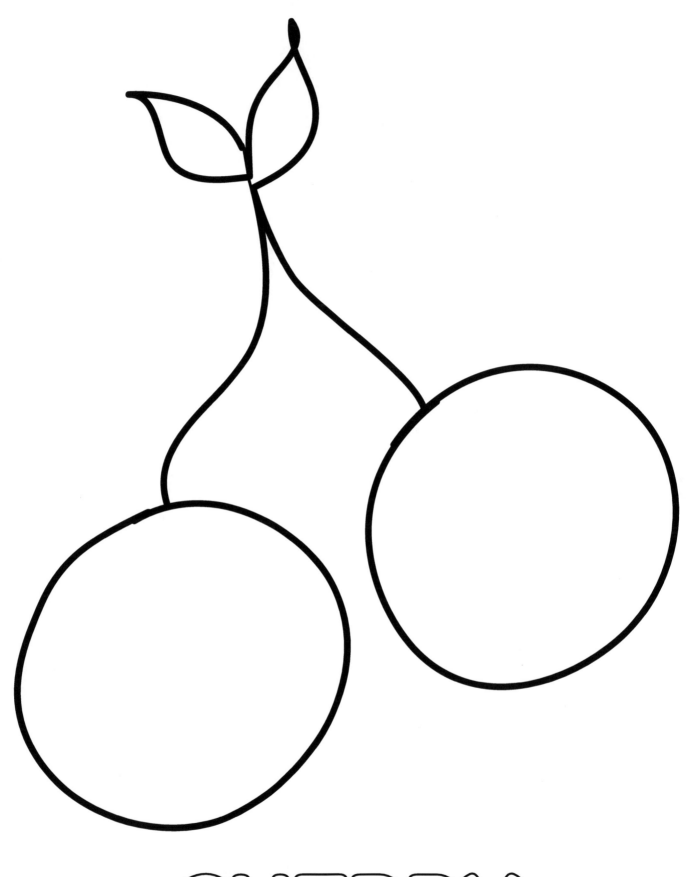

CHERRY

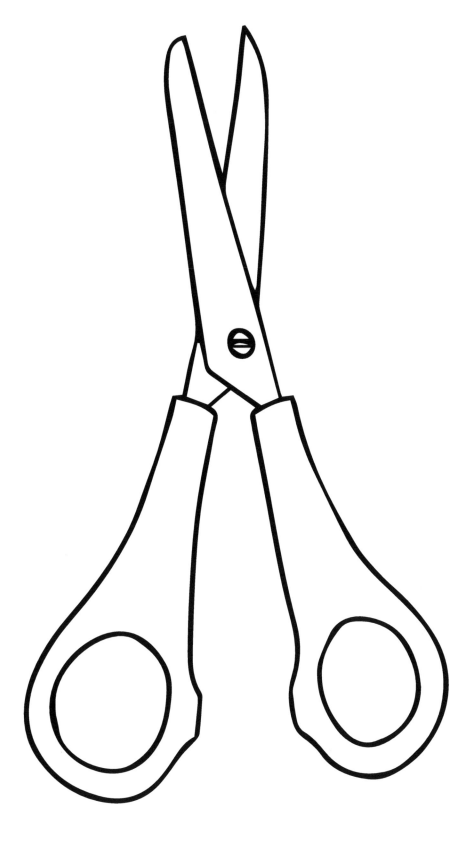

SCISSORS

TREE

BANANA

FROG

MANGO

DUCK

BLUEBERRY

CACTUS

ORANGE

BEANS

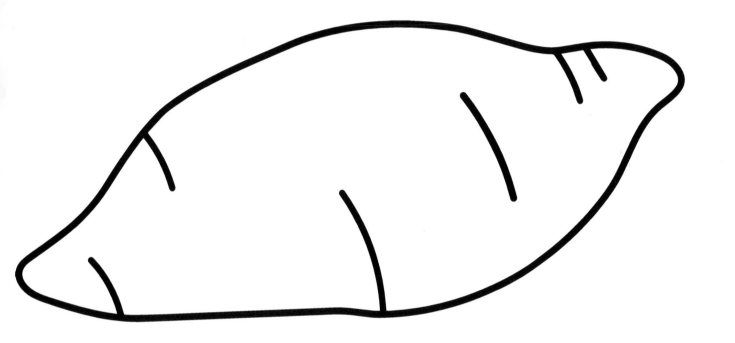

SWEET POTATO

APPLE

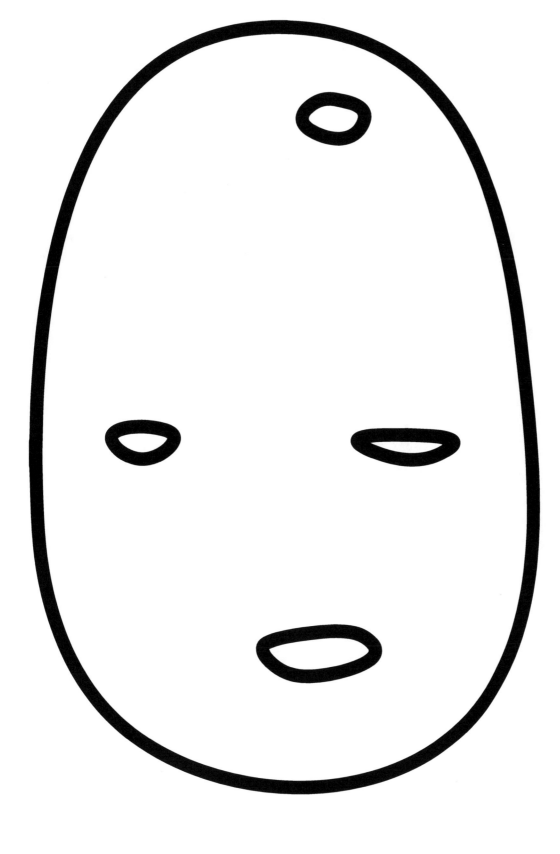

POTATO

FISH

ONION

PENCIL

LETTUCE

SUN

ICEBERG LETTUCE

CAULIFLOWER

GARLIC

HOUSE

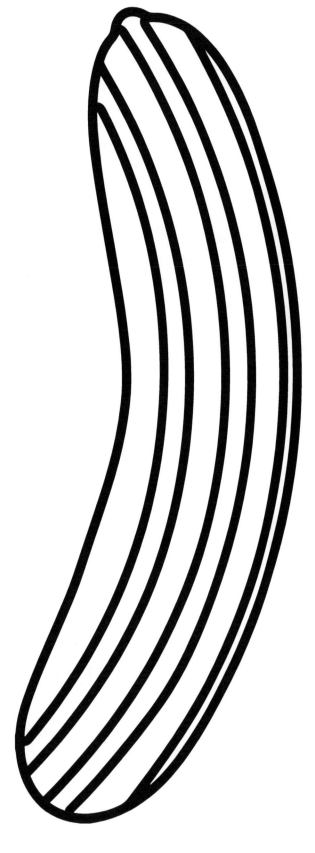

CUCUMBER

BEE

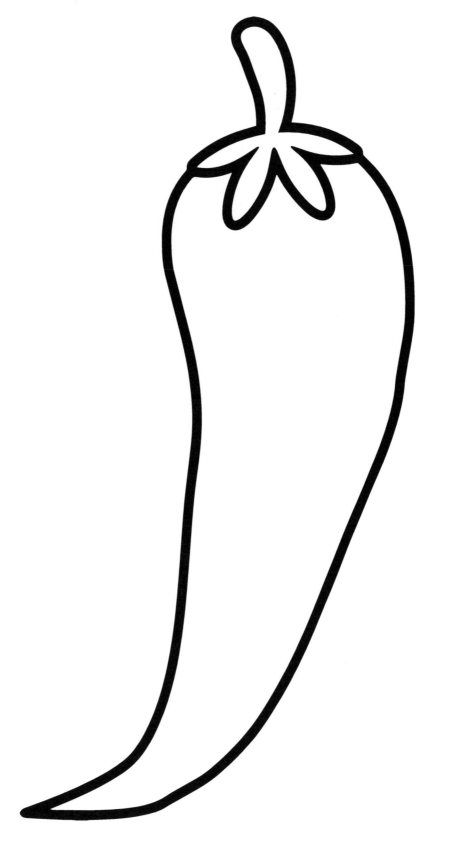

CHILI PEPPER

CLOCK

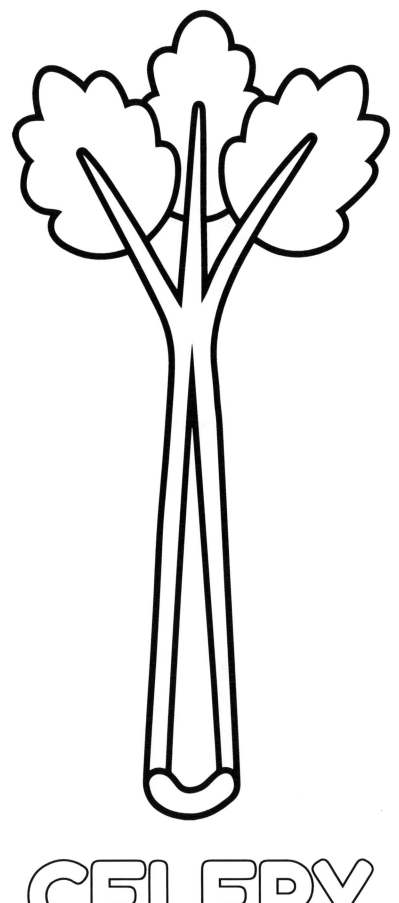

CELERY

LEAF

BROCCOLI

CAR

BELL PEPPER

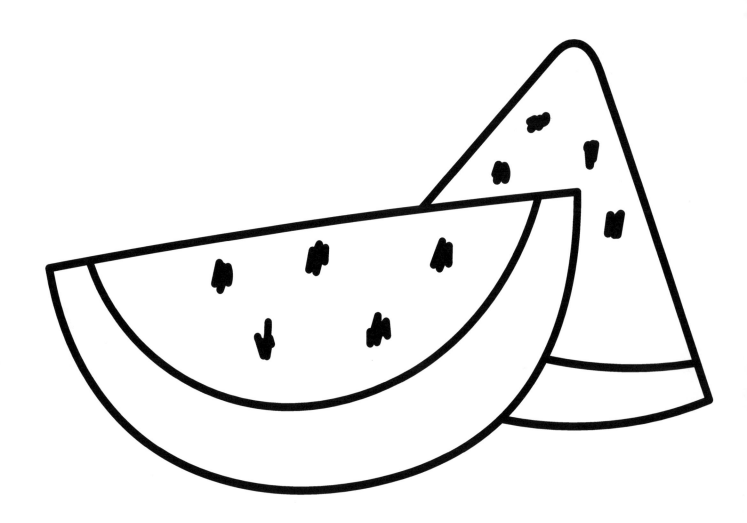

WATERMELON

BEET

PUMPKIN

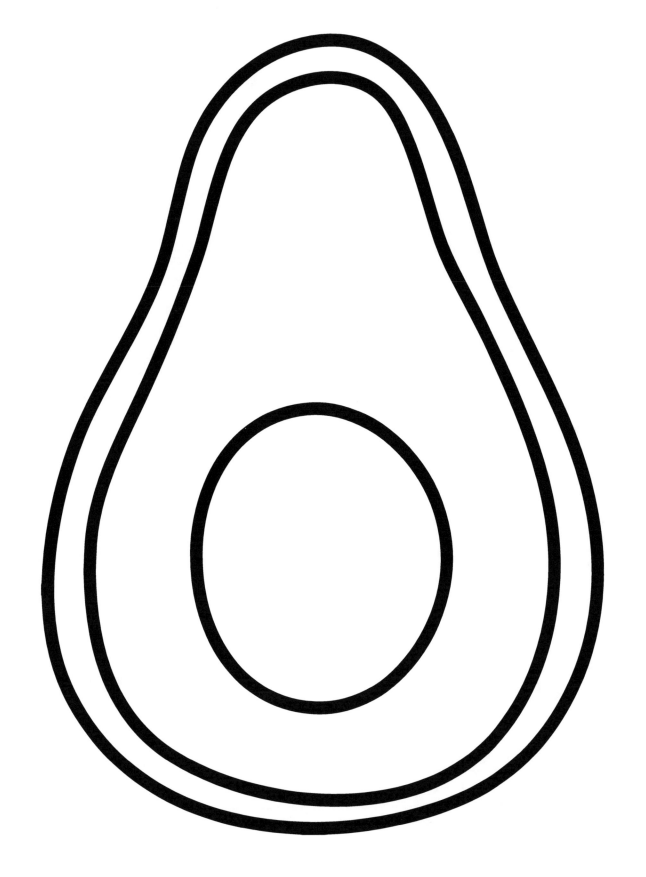

AVOCADO

TOY

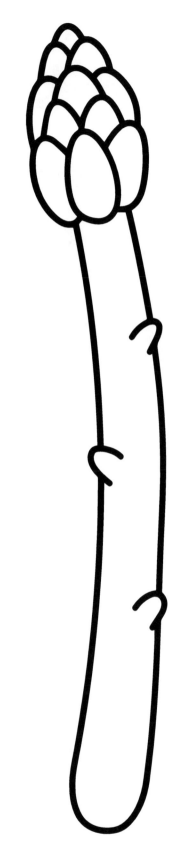

ASPARAGUS

BABY BOTTLE

TOMATO

ROCKET

CRAB

LION

PENGUIN

OWL

CANDY

BEAR

HEART

CAT

PIZZA

MUSHROOM

TACO

TURTLE

BURGER

KEY

BULB

WORM

MEGAPHONE

UMBRELLA

AIRPLANE

MOUSE

BALLOON

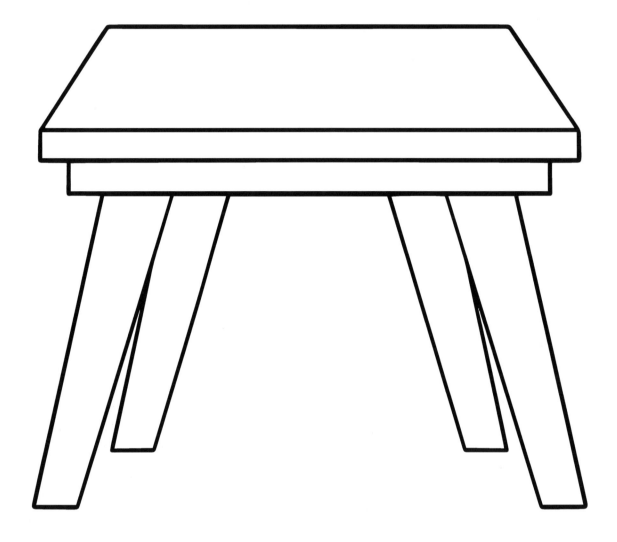

TABLE

DRUM

FOX

PARACHUTE

LAMB

CUP

HAT

TROPHY

Dear Customer
We produce all our books with love.
If you like this book, we would be very happy about an honest rating on Amazon.
Thank you very much for your purchase.

Imprint: S44 Invest GmbH
Zürcherstrasse 4, CH - 5620 Bremgarten
Tel: 0041 56 511 05 50 / info@s44.ch
USt-IdNr: DE345884896

Sales, Printing and Distribution: Amazon KDP or an affiliate.

Made in the USA
Las Vegas, NV
22 January 2024

84733840R10057